EXTREMELY Weird ANIMALS
STAR-NOSED MOLE

BY LISA OWINGS

BELLWETHER MEDIA • MINNEAPOLIS, MN

Jump into the cockpit and take flight with Pilot books. Your journey will take you on high-energy adventures as you learn about all that is wild, weird, fascinating, and fun!

This edition first published in 2014 by Bellwether Media, Inc.

No part of this publication may be reproduced in whole or in part without written permission of the publisher. For information regarding permission, write to Bellwether Media, Inc., Attention: Permissions Department, 5357 Penn Avenue South, Minneapolis, MN 55419.

Library of Congress Cataloging-in-Publication Data

Owings, Lisa.
  Star-nosed Mole / by Lisa Owings.
     pages cm – (Pilot. Extremely Weird Animals)
  Summary: "Engaging images accompany information about star-nosed moles. The combination of high-interest subject matter and narrative text is intended for students in grades 3 through 7"– Provided by publisher.
  Audience: Ages 7-12.
  Includes bibliographical references and index.
  ISBN 978-1-62617-078-0 (hardcover : alk. paper)
  1. Star-nosed mole–Juvenile literature. I. Title.
  QL737.S76O95 2014
  597.8′58–dc23
                          2013039381

Printed in the United States of America, North Mankato, MN.

TABLE OF CONTENTS

FEELING FOR FOOD

A star-nosed mole waddles through his dark underground tunnels in eastern North America. His tiny eyes are nearly useless, but he can "see" with his nose! It is surrounded by a blur of pink finger-like **tentacles**. They press into the dirt as he feels his way through the tunnels. Soon the tentacles close around a slick earthworm. The mole gobbles it up in an instant. Then he continues on his way.

The mole soon finds a tunnel opening. It reveals a shallow stream. The mole quickly jumps in and dives to the bottom. He feels along with his tentacles. When he thinks he has found a meal, he brings his nose close to it. He blows air bubbles out to touch it. Then he sniffs them back in. He smells dinner! The mole quickly swallows his meal. Then he returns to his tunnels to rest.

LIFE UNDERGROUND

Moles are small **mammals** that tunnel underground throughout Asia, Europe, and North America. They are part of a larger group of mammals that eat mainly insects. Moles make up the family Talpidae. The star-nosed mole is the only member of the **genus** Condylura. Its nose makes it different from any other mole or mammal.

human

star-nosed mole

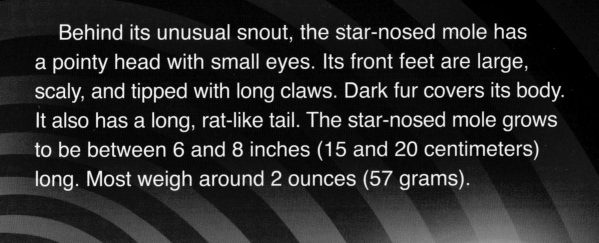

Behind its unusual snout, the star-nosed mole has a pointy head with small eyes. Its front feet are large, scaly, and tipped with long claws. Dark fur covers its body. It also has a long, rat-like tail. The star-nosed mole grows to be between 6 and 8 inches (15 and 20 centimeters) long. Most weigh around 2 ounces (57 grams).

Sticky Stars

When a star-nosed mole is born, its tentacles are folded backward and stuck to its face. It takes several days for them to peel away and spring forward.

Star-nosed moles live in southeastern Canada and the northeastern United States. They prefer moist soils in forests or near lakes, rivers, and wetlands. The moles use their front feet to dig long tunnels up to 2 feet (0.6 meters) underground. They move through the tunnels in search of insect **larvae** and earthworms.

Canada

United States

Mexico

star-nosed mole range =

Unlike other moles, star-nosed moles do much of their hunting underwater. They swim easily and snack on larvae, leeches, **shellfish**, and small fish. Star-nosed moles also **forage** above ground more often than other moles. At night, they follow the trails other small animals have made through tall grasses. The star-nosed mole's prey is usually small and not very rich in **nutrients**. Moles must spend a lot of time eating to get the energy they need.

Full-time Foragers

Searching for food is a full-time job for star-nosed moles. They can eat their own weight in food each day!

Star-nosed moles do not need to rely on daylight to hunt for prey. They are blind and spend most of their time underground. These moles are active both during the day and at night. About half their time is spent resting. Star-nosed moles dig cozy nests inside their tunnels for sleeping and raising their young. They often build these nests in dry places where their tunnels pass beneath logs. They line their nests with leaves or grass. Star-nosed moles mate in the spring. About six weeks later, females give birth to up to seven young.

Star-nosed moles are easy prey for many predators. Hawks and owls can snatch them from the ground. Skunks, foxes, and weasels also hunt star-nosed moles. Minks, large fish, and even bullfrogs can catch star-nosed moles while they are swimming. Most moles are thought to survive for three or four years in the wild.

Stay with the Group

Star-nosed moles are thought to live in small groups called colonies. Mated pairs share the same tunnels. Their relatives likely dig their tunnels nearby.

TENTACLES, TUNNELS, AND TAILS

This mole's star-shaped nose looks like something that lives at the bottom of the sea. It has 22 pink tentacles of different lengths. The tentacles are covered in tiny bumps called **Eimer's organs**. These organs are highly sensitive to touch. They can easily feel every tiny ridge and spike of an earthworm. Most mole species have 1,000 to 2,000 of these organs. The star-nosed mole has about 25,000! That makes the mole's nose about six times more sensitive than the human hand.

The mole's super-sensing star moves so quickly that human eyes can hardly follow it. Its waving tentacles can touch as many as 12 objects per second. As its tentacles touch an object, the mole decides instantly whether it can eat it. The process of touching, deciding to eat, and eating takes the star-nosed mole less than a quarter of a second. That makes it the fastest forager among mammals!

Feeling Good
The more excited a star-nosed mole is, the faster its tentacles move.

Touch is the star-nosed mole's most powerful sense. However, it also has a good sense of smell. It can even smell underwater! The star-nosed mole does this by breathing bubbles out of its nose until they touch an object. Then the mole quickly sucks the bubbles back in. The air inside the bubbles contains the object's smell. This gives the star-nosed mole another tool for finding food.

Scientists believe the star may help the mole find food in yet another way. They think the star can sense the faint **electric fields** of other animals through water. This may allow star-nosed moles to locate prey before they can touch or smell it. The star-nosed mole is likely the only mammal besides the platypus to have this ability.

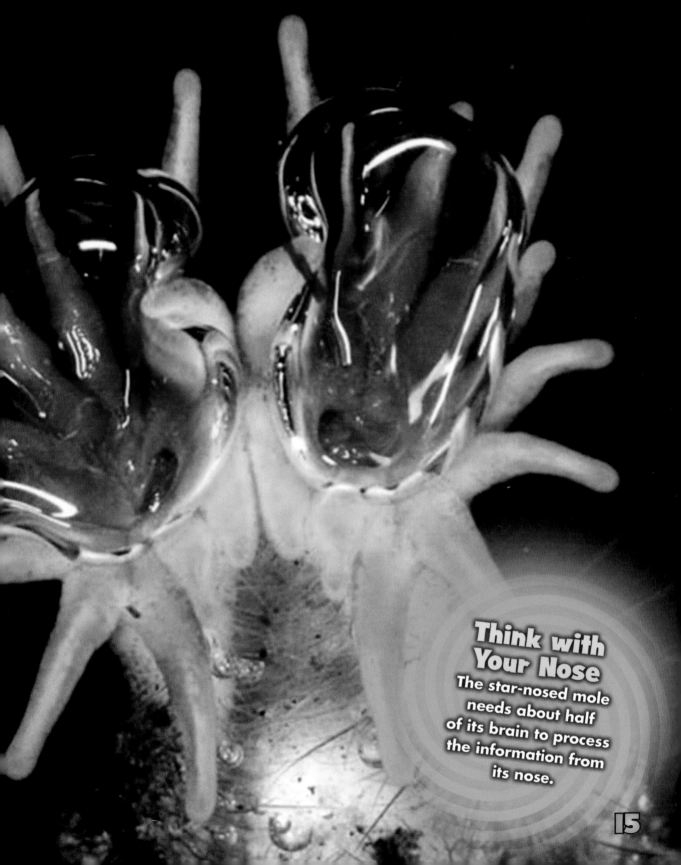

Think with Your Nose

The star-nosed mole needs about half of its brain to process the information from its nose.

15

The star-nosed mole's front feet look huge compared to its body. These hairless, scaly limbs end in long, sharp claws. The feet and claws are shaped like scoops to help the mole dig tunnels quickly. Its feet point sideways from its body, almost like fins. This makes a digging star-nosed mole look like it is swimming! Star-nosed moles can dig at least 7 feet (2 meters) of tunnel per hour. They push the loose dirt up to the surface to form large mounds near tunnel entrances.

Dirt Free

The star-nosed mole can fold its tentacles over its nose to keep dirt out while digging.

The mole's large front feet also help it move through the water. Their scoop-shaped claws act like paddles, making the star-nosed mole a strong swimmer. The mole moves in a zigzag pattern, stroking with one foot and then the other. Its tail helps it steer. The mole sticks its nose above the surface for air a few times each minute.

Little Helpers

Star-nosed moles help people by eating pesky insects. They also help plants grow by supplying the soil with air.

The star-nosed mole is well **adapted** to cold winters. Its dark fur grows thicker during the fall to help keep it warm. It does not need to tunnel deep into the earth during winter like many other moles. Instead, the star-nosed mole digs through the snow. It sometimes scurries along the surface.

It is harder for the star-nosed mole to find food in winter. Since the ground is frozen, the mole does most of its hunting underwater. It can often be found swimming beneath the ice. During the winter, the star-nosed mole's tail becomes up to four times thicker than in summer. The tail is used to store fat. This extra fat helps the mole get through the lean winter months. It also gives the mole enough energy for the spring **breeding** season.

SAFE FOR NOW

Star-nosed moles are **flourishing** in North America. They are common throughout their range in Canada and the United States. The number of star-nosed moles is holding steady, and they do not suffer from any major **threats**. They are currently listed as least concern. That means they are not in danger of becoming **extinct**.

However, the wetlands where star-nosed moles live are often drained to make way for homes and farms. This habitat loss may make it harder for them to survive in the future. Luckily, many star-nosed moles live in protected areas. For now, the moles and their star-shaped noses are safe inside their tunnels.

EXTINCT

EXTINCT IN THE WILD

CRITICALLY ENDANGERED

ENDANGERED

VULNERABLE

NEAR THREATENED

LEAST CONCERN

Star-nosed Mole
Fact File

Common Name:	star-nosed mole
Scientific Name:	*Condylura cristata*
Famous Feature:	star-shaped nose with 22 tentacles
Distribution:	southeastern Canada and the northeastern United States
Habitats:	moist soils near lakes, rivers, and swamps
Diet:	insect larvae, worms, shellfish, small fish
Life Span:	3 to 4 years
Current Status:	least concern

GLOSSARY

adapted—changed over time to adjust to a new situation

breeding—mating to produce young

Eimer's organs—tiny bumps on the skin that are highly sensitive to touch, pressure, and vibration; only moles have Eimer's organs.

electric fields—areas of energy around electrically-charged things

extinct—no longer existing as a species

flourishing—growing or doing very well

forage—to search for food

genus—a group of similar species

larvae—insects that have just recently been born or hatched

mammals—animals that have backbones, hair, and feed their young milk

nutrients—parts of food that provide energy

shellfish—hard-shelled animals that live mainly in water

tentacles—long, flexible parts of an animal that are often used for touching and grasping

threats—possible dangers

TO LEARN MORE

AT THE LIBRARY

Berger, Melvin, and Gilda Berger. *101 Freaky Animals*. New York, N.Y.: Scholastic, 2010.

Sebastian, Emily. *Moles*. New York, N.Y.: Rosen/PowerKids Press, 2012.

Spilsbury, Louise, and Richard Spilsbury. *Adaptation and Survival*. New York, N.Y.: Gareth Stevens, 2013.

ON THE WEB

Learning more about star-nosed moles is as easy as 1, 2, 3.

1. Go to www.factsurfer.com.

2. Enter "star-nosed moles" into the search box.

3. Click the "Surf" button and you will see a list of related Web sites.

With factsurfer.com, finding more information is just a click away.

INDEX

The images in this book are reproduced through the courtesy of: Minden Pictures/ SuperStock, front cover, p. 21; Ken Catania/ Visuals Unlimited/ Corbis, pp. 4-5, 6-7, 14-15; Dwight Kuhn, pp. 9, 10-11, 10, 13, 16-17, 17.